That Spark of Life -

Developing the Desire to Do Art

That Spark of Life -

of Life -

Developing the Desire to Do Art

Susan Oliver

ISBN 1542463963

Copyright © Susan Oliver 2013

Published in 2017

All artwork is done by the author.

Due to cost considerations, I have published this book in black-and-white. If you would like to see the artwork in colour, please go to my website:

http://suechantree.wixsite.com/soliverquilling

This book is comprised of a series of reflections to help you remember and to encourage your desire to do art.

It deals specifically with frustration around drawing and painting but, with a bit of imagination, it can be used for other arts and crafts and other activities as well.

Make this book your own and take your time with it. Always follow your gut.

I hope it is helpful to you.

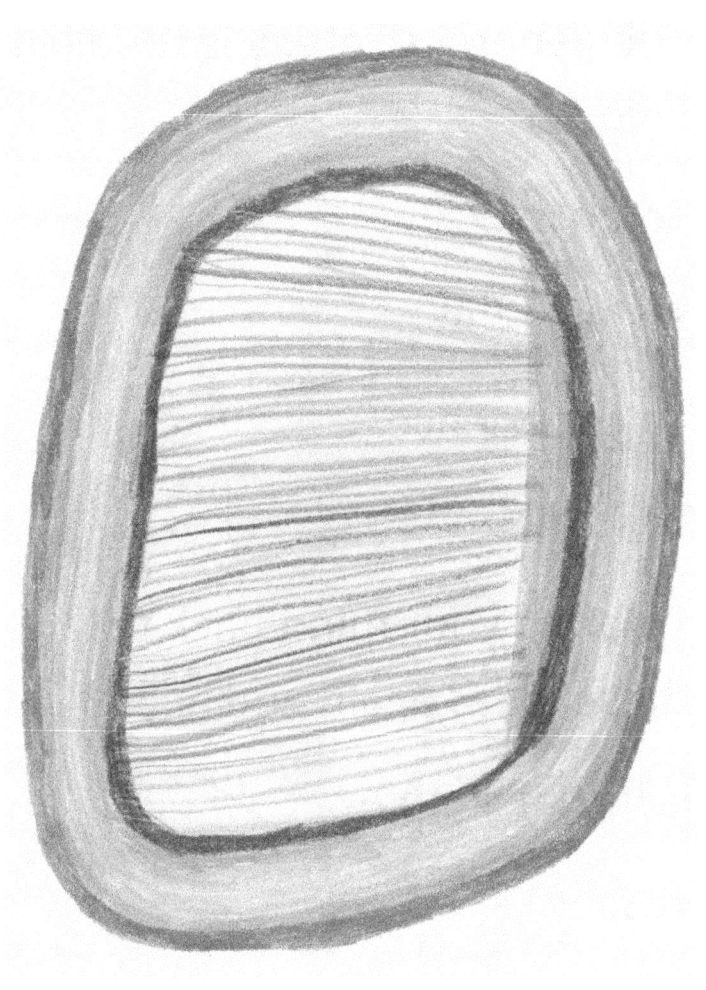

The general strategy is to fall in love.

To enjoy.

To have fun.

To experience.

That's it.

To bring your mind back to these ideas again and again.

Is it that simple?

Yes.

Ask yourself:

What would give me the most joy to draw now?

And now?

And now?

Move through time exploring this question.

And these:

What colour would give me the most happiness?

What shape is coming to me?

What image excites me?

What do I want to experience?

What am I curious about?

What do I care about?

How does my arm want to move?

It's about doing and loving, not thinking and judging.

You can't force the process.

Can you force yourself to dance?

Instead, you join with a spirit within to move and shift your body.

That is the way it is with art as well.

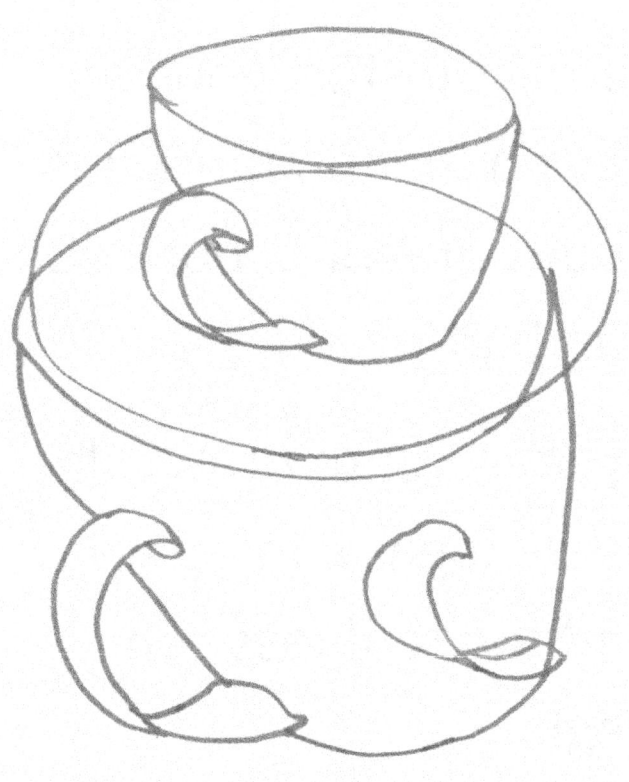

Until you start you can have a million fantasies about drawing, both good and bad.

By starting to draw, all those ideas can go away and the realness can begin.

It's not about preparation.

Or planning.

Or getting advice.

Or any kind of discipline.

It's about:

No pressures.

No anxieties.

No fear.

No worries.

No agendas.

No definitions.

No destinations.

It's about:

Relaxation.

Acceptance.

Patience.

Open-heartedness.

Gratitude.

Sincerity.

The joy of seeing.

The fun of using art materials.

The sweetness of using colour.

The happiness of doing.

The simplicity of being.

This isn't about avoiding discomfort or insecurities that may arise while drawing.

It's about questioning the concepts that cause discomfort and insecurity.

It's not about accomplishment because accomplishment entails pressure and comparison.

These ideas bring up fear which discourages you from doing anything.

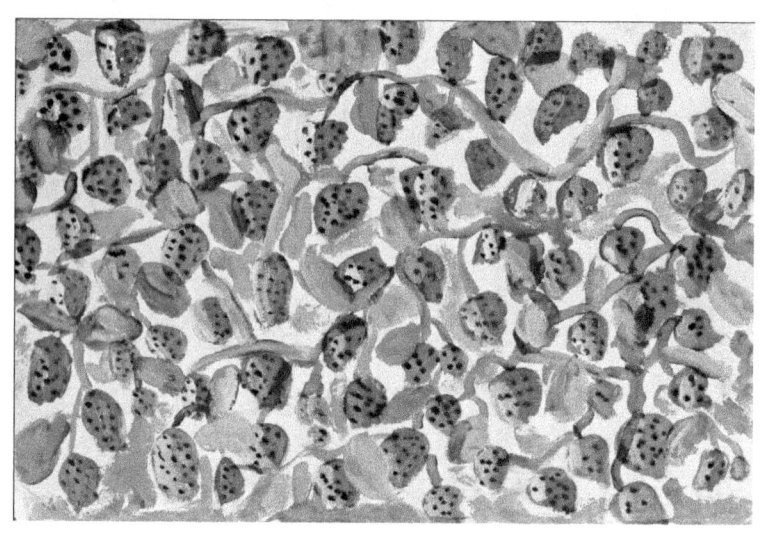

Fun-ness is a very powerful idea to focus on, especially in the early days.

Remind yourself, "I'm painting only to have fun, nothing else."

"I am here only to experience the love of drawing, the love of seeing, the love of form."

Or any other ideas like these that may come to you.

Let these ideas be your North Star, something to steer your ship by.

Another way to approach it is around peace.

"What would give me the most peace?"

"What is the most peaceful thing for me to do?"

Or, "What's the easiest thing to do?"

"What's the simplest thing to do?"

Don't wait for the perfect wave.

Accept what you have.

Do what you can.

Focus on your inner state while moving your implement on the paper.

Explore what is motivating you and what your feelings are like.

Feel how light-hearted you are and see if you can draw without any cares or worries.

How long can you draw as if you didn't have a care in the world?

Cultivate the idea that, on a piece of paper, you can do no wrong.

You may think, "I have to do this, I have to do that."

"I have to start a face at the eyes, I should draw nudes, I shouldn't use coloured pencils, I need to practice shadows..."

The mind can try to formulate a thousand rules.

This is about finding what you want to do without any rules or requirements.

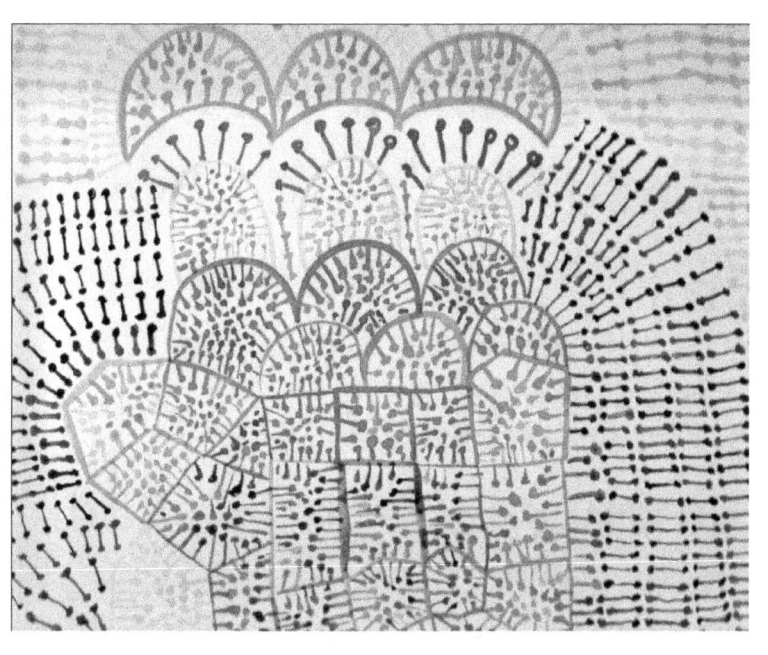

Think of art as a cat that you'd like to get close to.

Gently go near it, let it know you're interested.

Every once in a while during the day, go inside and softly ask yourself, "What do I feel like doing now?"

It's like asking, "What do I feel like eating?"

The answers may be very faint at first.

Be patient.

It can't be rushed.

Look around you and see if there's something that catches your fancy.

Is there an object that is calling you to draw it?

Is there anything you're particularly curious about?

Have you noticed a colour or a combination of colours that you like?

It may be a very subtle interest but any interest is a spark of life.

Become conscious of your sparks, no matter how insignificant they may seem.

Take note of any wisp of interest.

Acknowledge any small tug to draw.

Sparks can come in the following forms:

Images in your mind, including shapes.

Things in the world that attract you.

Ideas, feelings, hunches, inclinations.

Thoughts, questions & curiosities.

(cont'd...)

(...cont'd)

Colours you feel like experiencing.

What your arm feels like doing/how your body feels like moving.

And any other ways you get inspiration.

Be on the look-out for any artistic impulse that comes to you.

Don't feel badly if all you want to do is to draw squiggles or what may be called doodles.

Accept what you're inspired to do and concentrate on the positive thoughts and feelings you have when you draw.

The eyes can't see a
lot.

They can't perceive
the mystery behind a
doodle or the cosmic
force that creates a
squiggle.

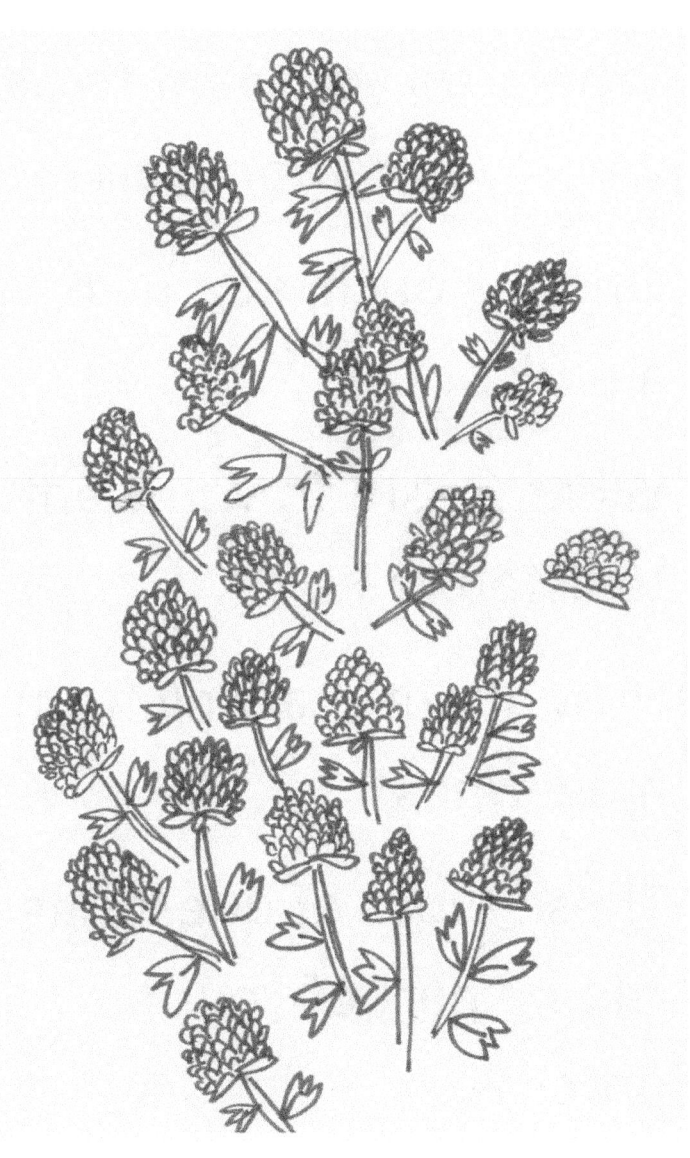

35

Where do you want to be when you're doing art?

On the couch, at a desk, in a park or café?

What music do you want to listen to?

How about drawing from magazines?

These types of questions can be part of your process.

Where on the paper do you want to start?

It's the place that excites you the most or is the easiest place to start.

It's the place that YOU want to start, not based on stories or formulas you've heard but based on your own internal guidance.

How fast do you want to draw?

How slow? How accurately?

Careful, messy, haphazard, bold, delicate, thick, thin, broad strokes, tiny strokes.

Some of the image, all of it.

On top of the paper, on the bottom, in the middle, all around.

How much concentration do you want to use?

Do you want to be intense and deliberate?

Or relaxed and casual?

These are different promptings that may come to you and no artistic urge is insignificant.

There's no need to be fancy.

You're not out to impress anybody or prove anything.

Shoot for honesty, sincerity.

Repetition is 100% okay.

If you feel like repeating an image, go for it.

Don't worry about completing a drawing.

Do only that much that you want to do.

For example, if you only feel inclined to draw certain parts of a building or perhaps just the feeling it gives you, welcome and do that.

Don't put any pressure on yourself to produce a picture or to make a statement.

No care should be given to anything unless you want to give it. This includes matters of colour, form, balance and composition.

Don't worry about what you don't want to do.

Focus on what you *do* want to do.

Finish when you want to, when you feel like it's time, when you feel at peace to do so.

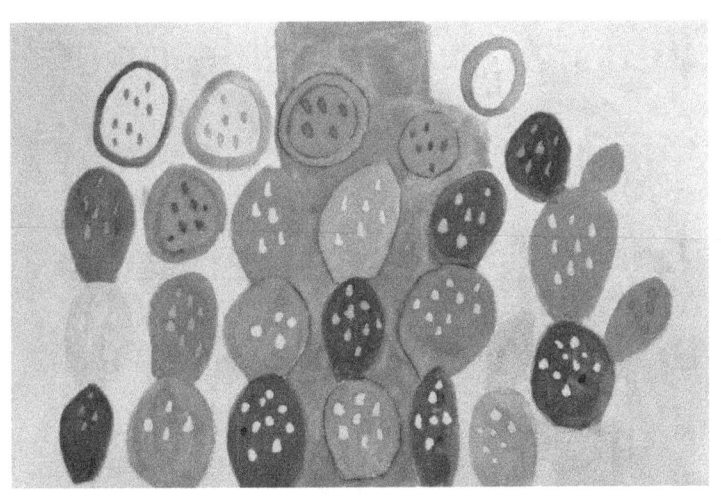

Think of the idea of decorating like you were decorating a cookie or a cake.

Try to feel that freedom and joy - that glee! – that comes with decorating and apply it to drawing.

Feel it also when you use colour.

Cultivate a friendship with colour with no agenda to master it.

Don't feel that you need to understand colour or study colour theory in order to enjoy it.

Use the colours you love.

If you have trouble choosing colours, reduce the number of choices and get familiar with one colour at a time. As you become comfortable with a few, slowly increase the number of options.

"What colour do I want to experience?" is another good way to approach it.

Sometimes it's fun to pick out colours at random.

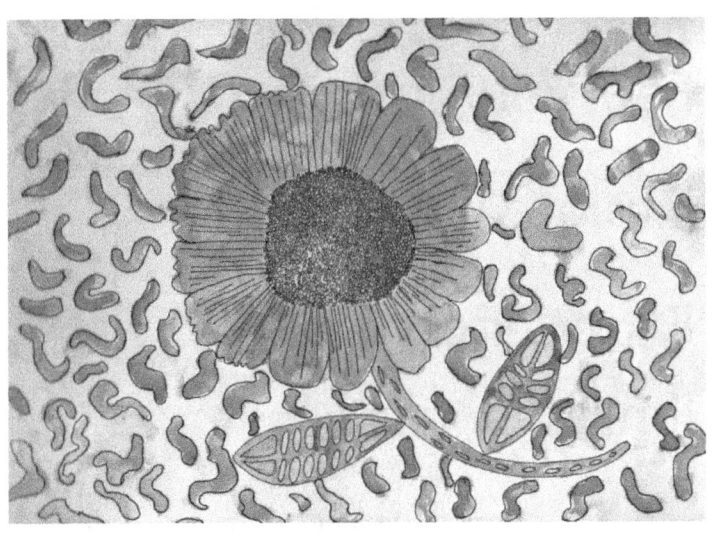

Doing art gives you a wonderful opportunity to:

Feel your infinity.

Explore your freedom.

Experience your limitlessness.

...in a world where there are many inherent limitations.

Drawing and painting enables you to get closer to the world around you.

Look around. What do you want to get near to?

You may also be inspired to draw from your imagination.

You may have times when you don't feel like drawing.

You get a strong feeling of, "Nope, not today."

Respect that.

This is a highly personal process and you need to become your own teacher.

You may also experience strong feelings about what *not* to draw.

Those are important, too.

A single step in a true direction is worth more than a thousand steps in a false one.

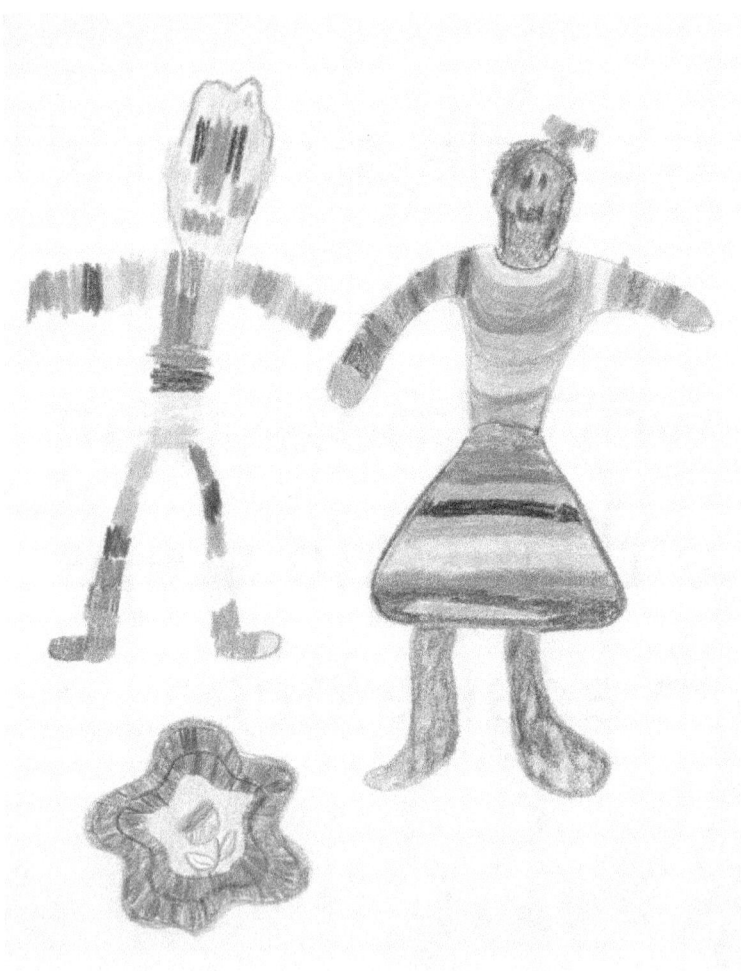

While you are drawing
you are discovering
what you like to
experience, see and do.
It is through making
these discoveries that
your style emerges.

Trust where the adventure is taking you.

Courage is necessary at times.

You have to stick up for your authenticity.

You need to stick up for your genius.

Make the obvious choices first.

Do the easiest thing.

The decisions that come without strain, without effort – these are the choices that are most "you."

As you keep drawing and painting, don't be concerned if a work looks "worse" than a previous one.

Never worry about "regressing."

This is a very mysterious process and progress does not happen in a straight line.

Get to know what your motivation feels like, its ebbs and flows.

Notice anything new that arises. Appreciate small developments.

Take special notice of when you are positive toward your work, even if you can't put your finger on what you like or if it's something very minor.

Become very
sensitive to what
makes you
happy.

Sometimes just seeing is enough.

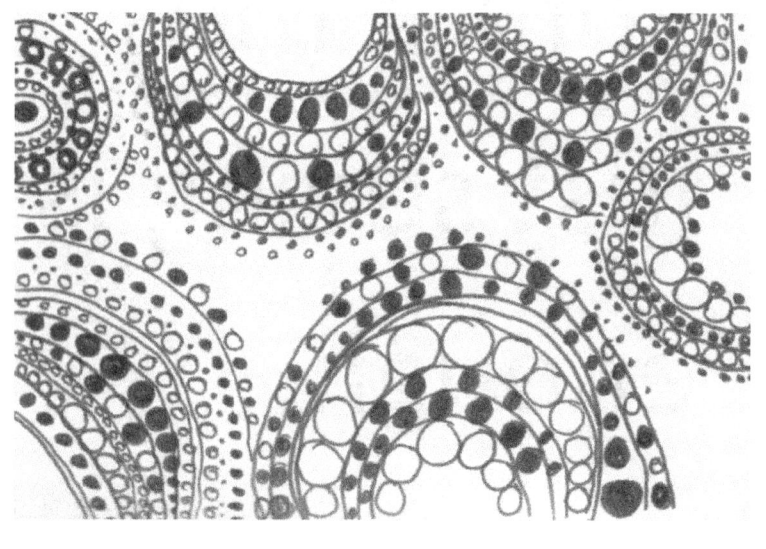

Part of the mind will try to assess the worth of your drawings.

It does this by comparing them to a million other drawings or artistic concepts in a flash of an instant.

The mind compares so much in the effort to find out what's "best and better" that it forgets that creation is the only goal.

Comparing works of art against each other is done by a mind that is not fully convinced it's all about love.

If you want to compare your work with anything, compare it with a blank piece of paper.

Anything is better than nothing at all.

The fact that you are drawing is the miracle and the true value of what you draw can never be calculated.

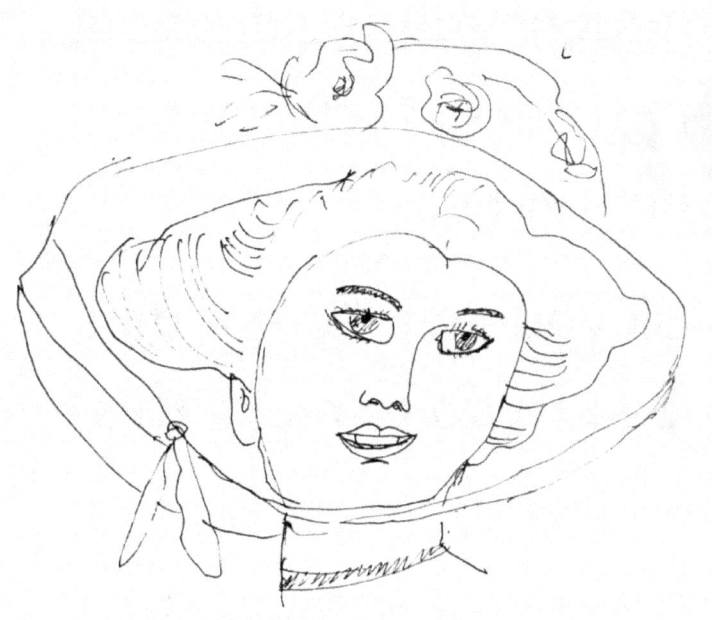

When you have negative thoughts during drawing, try to keep focusing on the fun-ness.

Ask yourself, "What do I need to do to make this fun again?"

Sometimes a new colour can help.

Sometimes it's a sign to stop for the day.

It can be humbling to draw something and have it not look like the real thing.

The mind can be very tough, very judgmental.

Thankfully, this tendency gradually submits to the wisdom of the process.

Another doubt is the idea that a drawing looks like a child's.

It's actually a great gift to draw with the freedom of a child.

You may come to points during a drawing where you feel fear, like you're going to make a mistake or spoil a piece or do something that may be considered unsophisticated, out-of-date or a host of other negative adjectives.

You've reached a place in your mind where you are reliant on being right. You've created a formula for success.

It's a place where you are particularly harsh with yourself.

Can you ever really be "wrong" in art?

Or is it just that you're going in a different or new direction?

Try to keep going despite the fear.

It's the pull of right/ wrong and good/bad that we need to go beyond.

Memories may surface while you are drawing.

Anger, too, may be experienced.

These are ways the mind is trying to heal itself.

It's de-tangling.

Constellations are being simplified.

A lot is being released.

Be gentle with yourself as issues and fears are brought to the surface.

Doing art gives you a safe place to look at your fears.

It gives you an opportunity to look at your own mind.

This can be difficult but, in the long run, it's a shortcut to learning what we all need to learn.

Concentrating on what you love requires a level of mental energy you may not be used to so you may feel tired after a short time.

You're using larger gears so be careful you don't get too tired.

Take breaks. You may need to go to sleep earlier, too.

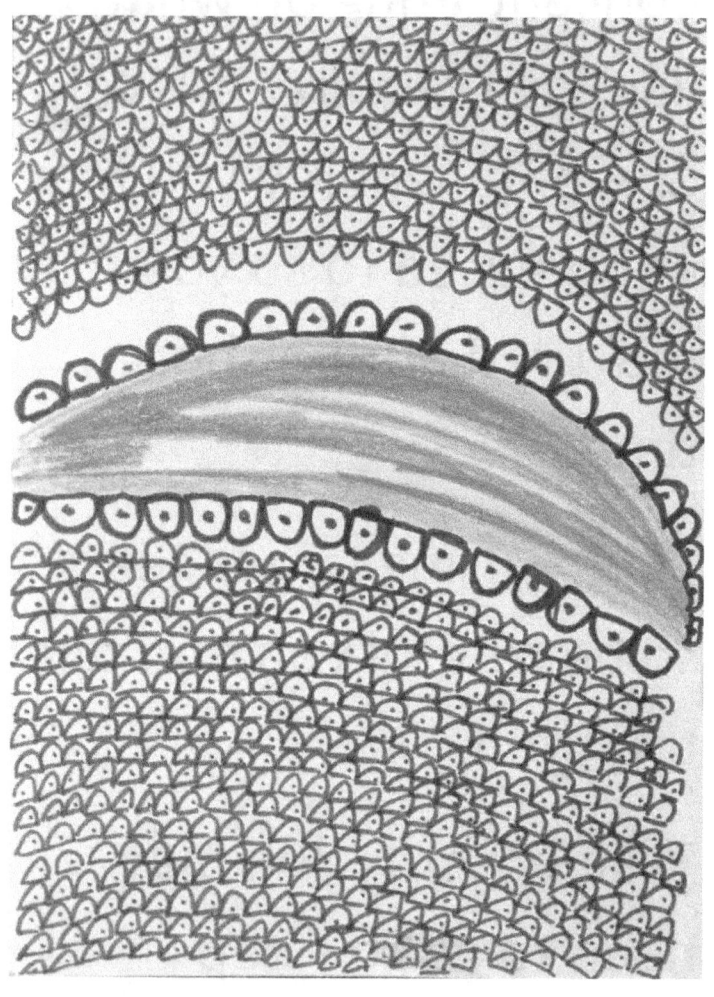

If you feel the impulse to take a class, by all means go for it. Trust your instincts.

But don't "hang your hat" on it.

In other words, don't think it's going to give you what you really want, which is your passion, your desire to do art.

It's seductive to think that a certain technique or a special teacher is going to be the answer.

A technique or teacher can help but they can't create your inner motivation.

Art supplies can be
another thing we hope
will inspire us.

Supplies are inanimate
objects and the high of
buying them quickly
wears off.

Shopping can be used as an attempt to fill an inner void.

Do art instead and experience real satisfaction.

Focus on doing rather than having.

See the materials
as a means to
open your heart.

Too much stuff can be a distraction so it may be helpful to sell or give away supplies that are no longer needed.

Deciding what art or craft you focus on is very personal but falling in love is ultimately the key.

That spark of life works through any medium or activity.

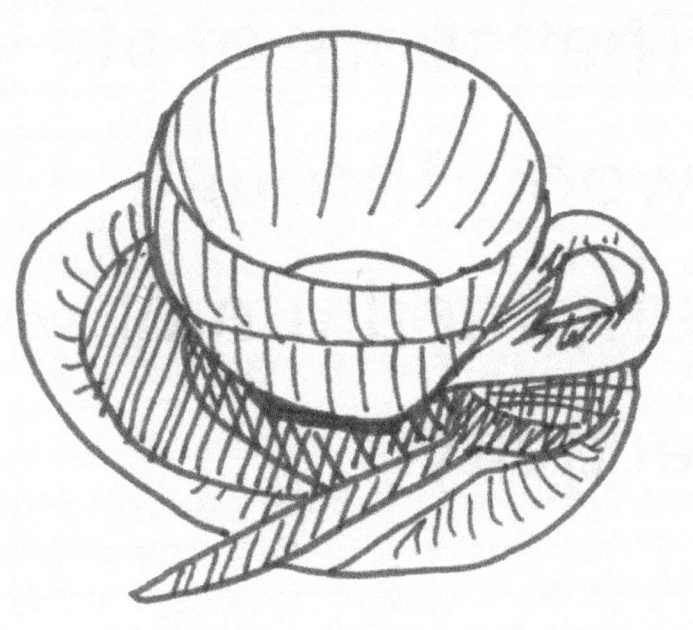

Detail is something that can bring up a lot of fear.

This can feel like a sense of defeat at the complexity of a subject before you even start.

"How am I going to put in every blade of grass and leaf on a tree?" one may ask.

Seek for inspiration when you look at the world.

Intimidation is the
opposite of inspiration.

If you are feeling
intimidated, remember
the basic strategy of
focusing on what you love
and drawing that.

It's easy to forget when
faced with something new
or something with a lot of
detail like a landscape.

We can have a lot of opinions about detail. These are based on stories of what's right and wrong.

Let all those opinions go and put in only what you are inspired to do, even if it's only a little.

If we force ourselves to put in detail, we're eventually going to associate art with misery and work.

If you find yourself going into seriousness when doing something small or fiddly, remember the idea of fun.

Detail comes from loving what you see and enjoying what you do.

It needs to blossom in its own season.

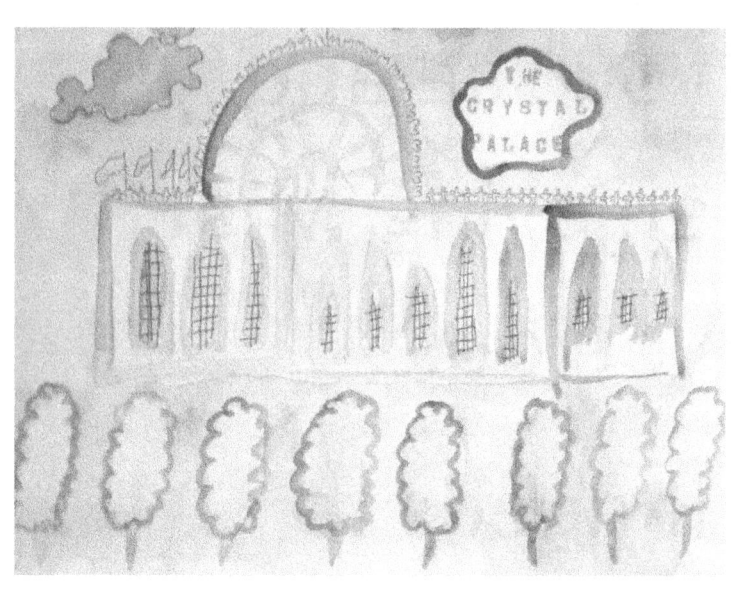

Skill can
easily
become a
false god.

What is skill?

It's usually associated with stories of what's important, of what counts for good in the world.

It's also a belief in levels and the ability to go up and down those levels.

So it's based in comparison.

Comparison and judgement don't help you find what you love.

The ideas of skill and improvement quickly create a sense of toil, which erodes your desire to do art.

In moments when you feel pulled by the idea of skill, think of art as a playground and just play.

Re-define skill as the ability to follow your heart.

It's an internal ability that no one can teach you except yourself but it's the most important.

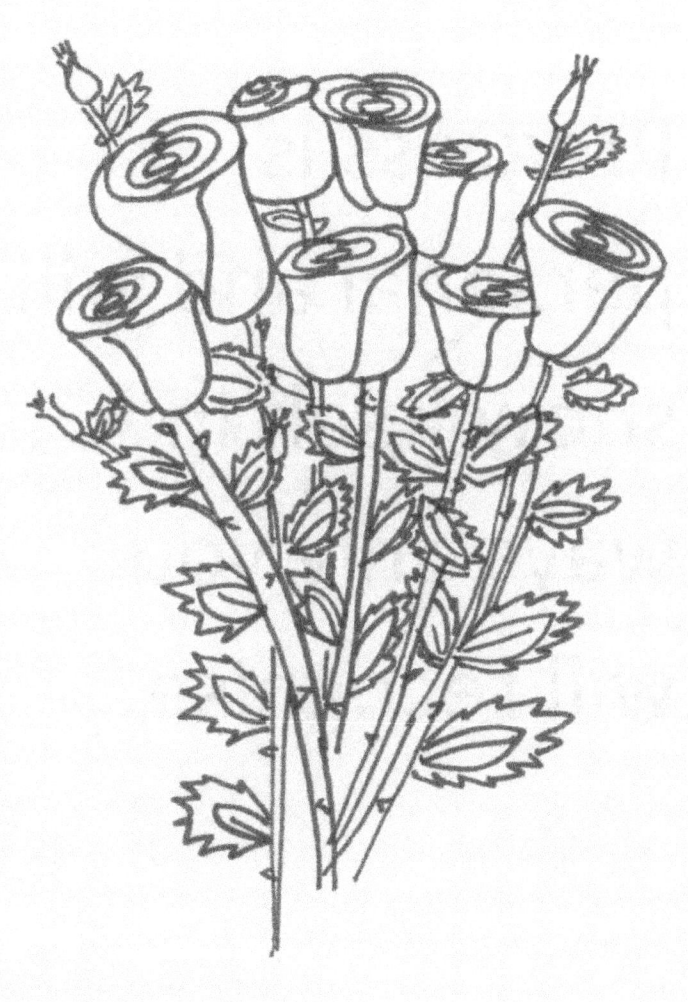

Progress is personal and will show itself in ways only you will recognise.

It's about developing an inner compass based on love rather than fear.

It takes a while to know which system you are relying on. Be kind to yourself as your instincts take hold.

You may be concerned about being stuck or that, without outside direction, you will wallow in nothingness.

You may experience feelings of meaningless-ness or a loss-of-centre as you adjust to a different way of doing things.

These are temporary.

You may go through phases.

You may be obsessed with drawing this or drawing that.

Maybe a certain image or style or an idea will stick for a while, and then you'll move on.

These, also, should be done without any judgments.

By keeping a light heart and being true to yourself, you learn integrity and authenticity. Your curiosity and ability to concentrate improve.

The questions and worries that kept you from painting are dealt with by the process itself.

All misunderstandings about what you want or need from art are worked through by doing it.

Art itself wants to teach you and lead you.

Give it a chance.

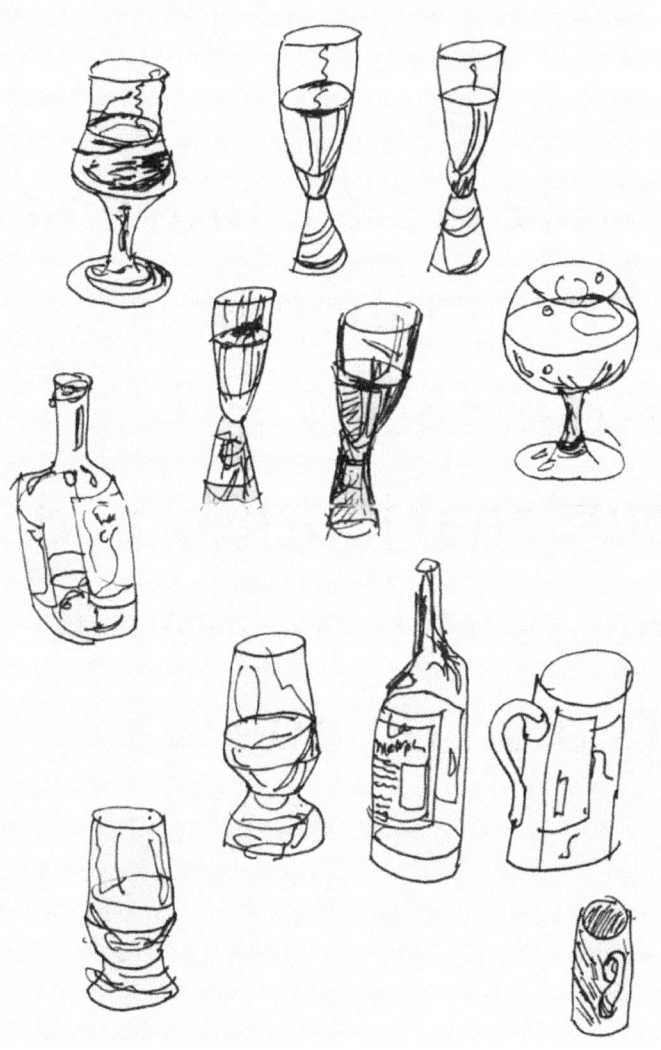

123

While art is a universal phenomenon, it is experienced as a personal journey and yours will manifest in its own unique way.

This may mean finding and giving up unconscious ambitions about our drawing or painting.

What expectations do we *really* harbour?

Ambition can be ruthless and foster unrealistic goals.

It can also make us doubt our inspiration, our inner guide, for temporary satisfaction.

The conflict between ambition and inspiration can often be felt around the idea of a "finished work," or something we'd like to share with other people either informally or in a formal setting like a gallery.

We may feel pressured to create something special to show.

We may feel the need to create something extraordinary, like pulling a rabbit out of a hat.

Showing our work involves being comfortable with what we're creating.

So instead of preparing out-of-the-ordinary pieces, the work should reflect what is being produced on a regular basis.

There is no need to rush this stage before its time.

Art itself will tell you when it should happen.

The desire to show your work is going to come from a continued art practice.

And a long-term relationship with art will provide you with the kindest and trustiest Sherpa you will ever find.

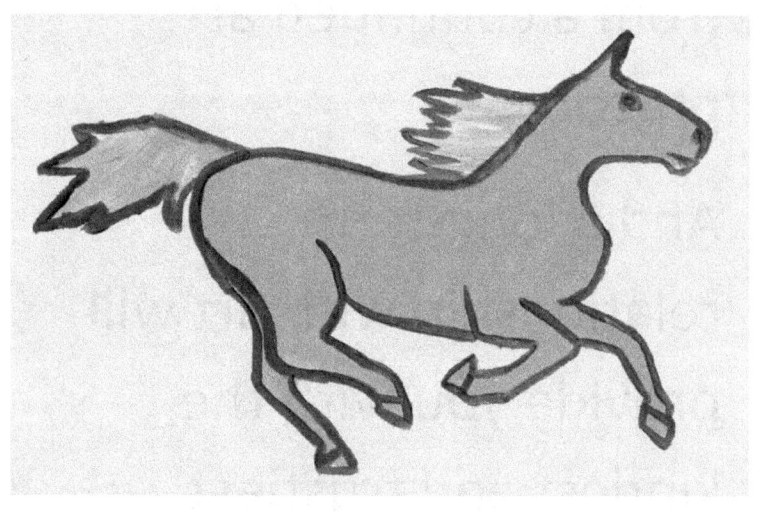

This method is not about banning judgment.

It's about using it appropriately and reasonably.

Judgment should serve love, not the other way around.

Drawing and painting give you a chance to look at and soften any tendencies to "figure things out."

Too often we let the mind set the direction and force the heart to follow.

This journey is about allowing the heart to set the direction and asking the mind to serve the heart.

The heart knows how to love so we need to leave scrutiny behind for a long time in order to give it our full dedication.

The heart serves as a flashlight; it shows you what to care about.

Caring creates the motivation to draw, which then gives you something else to care about and explore.

This becomes the pump for doing art, not planning, intellectual understanding, or getting validation.

Art knows where you have been relying on old, unhelpful ideas that were learned long ago and will ask you to slowly give these up so that you can make up fresh ideas and use your own creativity.

There is no end to this freshness.

Judgement can also be used for self-protection or self-promotion, which means doing things that we know will probably get approval or attention.

It's a sure road to artistic contraction because it uses up a lot of energy and takes you down a maze of fear.

"Am I approaching this from love or fear?" is a good question to ask.

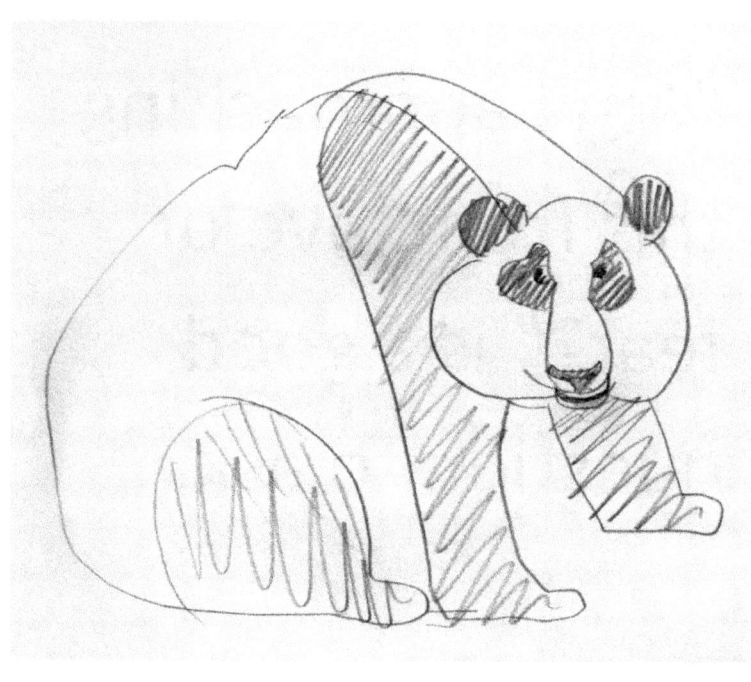

This is a long-term project and it doesn't happen overnight.

Think of it as a practice, a life-style, a pilgrimage.

Other people may not understand what you are doing.

They may not appreciate your work so don't feel pressured to show your sketchbooks to anyone if you don't want to.

You also may find that you don't "like" what you create. That's normal.

There is a gentle re-training of the mind that occurs during this process.

Over time, the mind becomes quieter and starts to judge less. It becomes more accepting and starts to see value in little things here, little things there.

Developing and trusting a set of artistic hunches takes time.

It's all about perception.

Wrong becomes "Why not?"

5,000 "mistakes" and then the one action that makes you realise, "That's my style!"

It's all about doing it – and keeping on doing it.

And the only way to do this is to have fun doing it, to associate drawing with fun, joy, and happiness at every turn.

Concentrating on these qualities will shape your mind and motivations more than anything else.

The *desire* to draw is your most valuable asset. That is why the strategy is based on cultivating that.

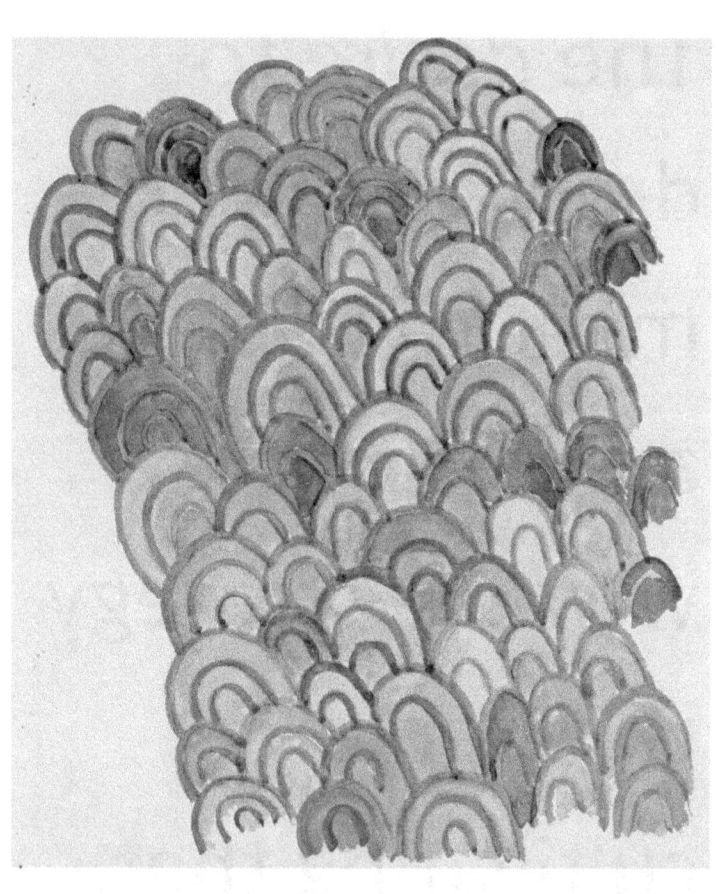

What everyone is really looking for in art is a unique and consistent style.

This is the artist's individuality being expressed and celebrated.

Thankfully, your style is uncovered as you develop a living connection with art.

It's like finding your creativity and genius and joy all in one pill.

It's one-stop shopping for everything you really want.

Your style comes from a much deeper place than wanting to draw a pretty picture or to be successful.

It's a mysterious process that can't be rushed or thought-through but it's worth it.

You get to a place where you don't care about other people's opinions.

Your connection with art becomes so strong that you're simply not interested in what other people think.

You're also not interested in being anyone else but yourself.

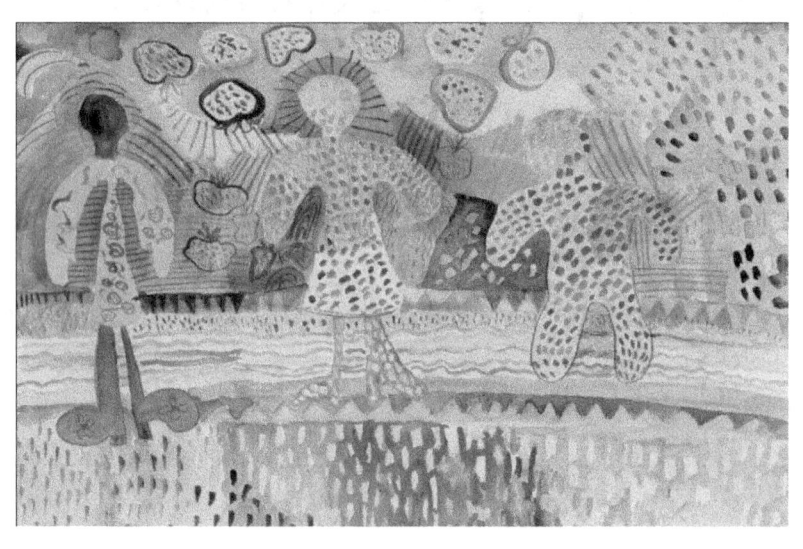

Artistic jealousy
is a sign that
you're longing for
your own
connection with
art.

It can be disheartening to see other people's accomplishments, especially at moments when we are discouraged with our own work.

It's a time for faith and a call *not* to be pulled in by the grip of wanting to be something – or somebody – we're not.

Be aware of what you are wanting – recognition, fame, financial success or to have some kind of ability, etc.

Realise these are knocking on your door to trick you into abandoning the goal of having a relationship with art.

Forgive any desire to be like "so and so" — one of the masters or whoever you think is more skilled or more whatever.

You first have to be yourself.

There can also be a tendency to be defeatist, to look at other's pictures and think, "What's the point when there are so many people - living and passed - more 'advanced' than me?"

One could easily think that when walking around a museum.

All the museums and all the masterpieces in the world can't compete with the value of you doing your own art because the value is in the doing it.

Doing art allows you to experience your own inner beauty and we all need and deserve that.

It shows you how beautiful YOU are.

Eventually, when you are committed to your own vision, other peoples art feels like a distant cousin. So jealousy fades away and you are reminded of how grand love is.

You become more appreciative of work no matter what it looks like and it all feels like one big family.

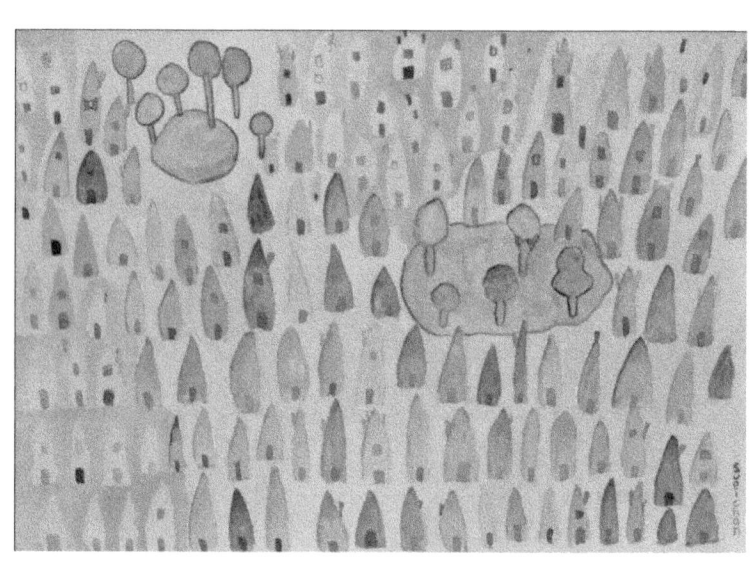

Pessimism arises when we feel like we're not getting what we want.

We slide into pessimism easily because we have been trained to believe in "getting" more than in simple enjoyment.

Pessimism is a two-step process based in the idea of lack: "I don't have _____ so I feel like I'm lacking (and I'm going to be discouraged.)"

Relieving pessimism is also a two-step process:

1. Identify what you think you're not getting.
2. Concentrate on the positives that you *are* experiencing.

Identifying what you think
you're not getting is
helpful because the
frustration doesn't remain
a mystery anymore.
The issue is brought into
awareness so it becomes
less fearful and easier to
heal.

Focusing on the positive is *especially important* when you feel pessimistic.

Find *any speck(s)* of satisfaction in your practice and cling onto them like they were more valuable than gold because, in this process, they are.

Concentrate on any joy in your mind like you were trying to taste it.

If comparison is part of the problem, take a temporary break from looking at other people's art.

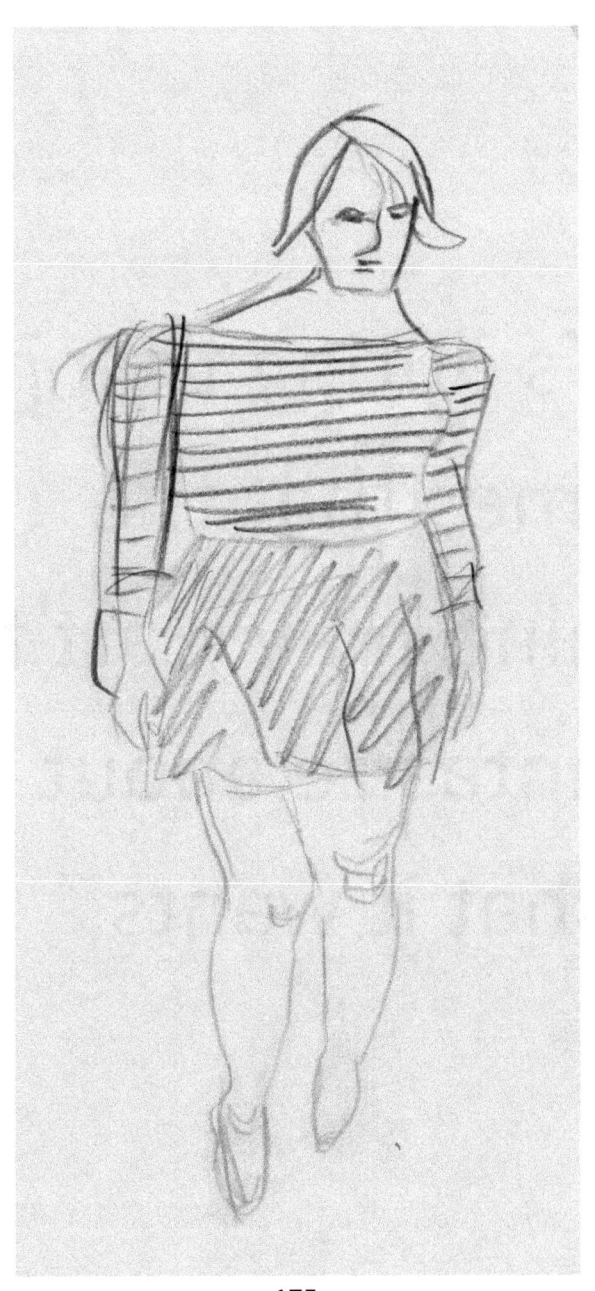

175

It's during trying times that the mind may start to fantasize about what it wants.

It looks for short-cuts and easy formulas to be "good" because it wants outer validation or to re-gain control over the process.

There may also be a tendency to be future-oriented, to make plans and think about big projects and endeavours in order to avoid an emptiness that the mind *assumes* it is being presented with.

By continuing to do art, these tendencies (that are created out of fear) start to subside and you are able to explore what is valuable to YOU in the PRESENT MOMENT.

You develop your own formulations of what "good" are, which are often surprising!

Art will open your head if you let it.

This will not only help your art but other areas of your life as well.

Art will challenge and change your perception.

It asks you to be open to new ideas of what is "good."

This open-mindedness enables a greater ability to perceive potential and be inspired.

Even if you do not impress other people, you will find value many other ways.

This inevitably will make you happy and isn't that the end goal anyway?

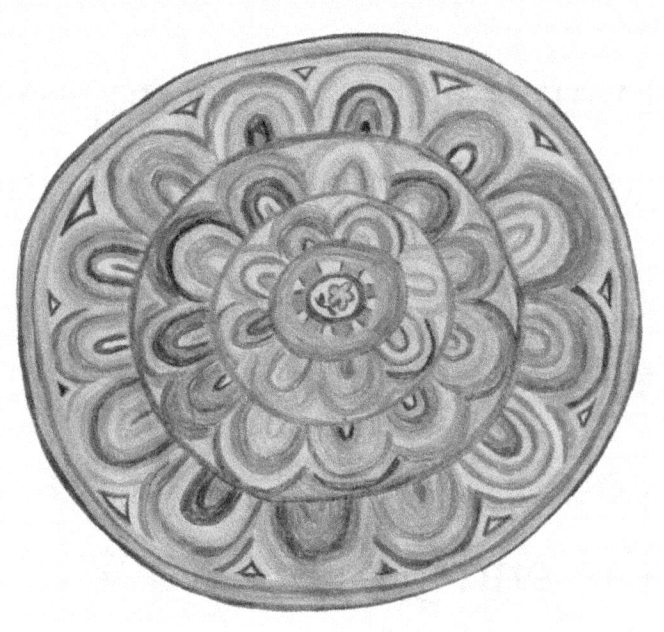

Healing does not
always happen in
a straight line.

You may be prompted to stop drawing for a long period of time, perhaps to concentrate on something else or for an unknown reason.

Even if it's been months – or years – since doing art, go within and ask yourself, "Is it time to begin again?"
Follow your inner directive.

Be compassionate with yourself if and when you come back to drawing.

Re-connect with the practice of going within and asking, "What do I feel like doing?"

Try not to go into regret or guilt.

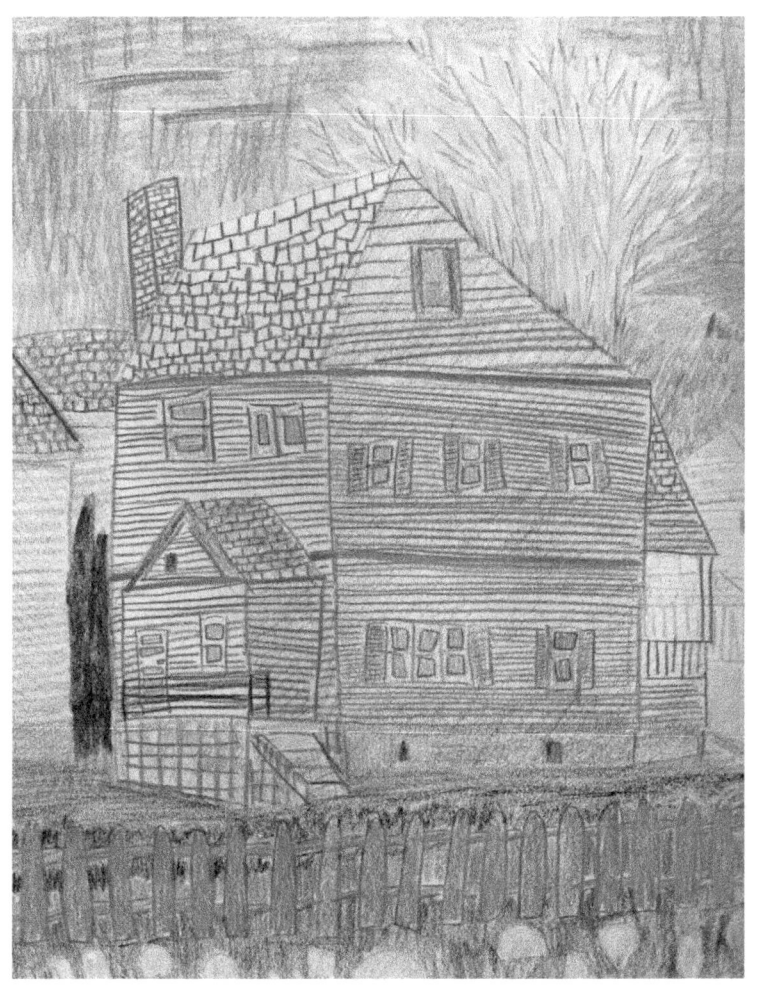

The energy behind the desire to draw is the limitless power of love.

Joy, curiosity, interest and fun – these are the backbone to any kind of passion.

Be grateful for your sparks of life – they are unique to you.

By appreciating your sparks, you are sustained by something deeper than praise or recognition.

It's like finding an inexhaustible fountain or a diamond mine the size of the earth.

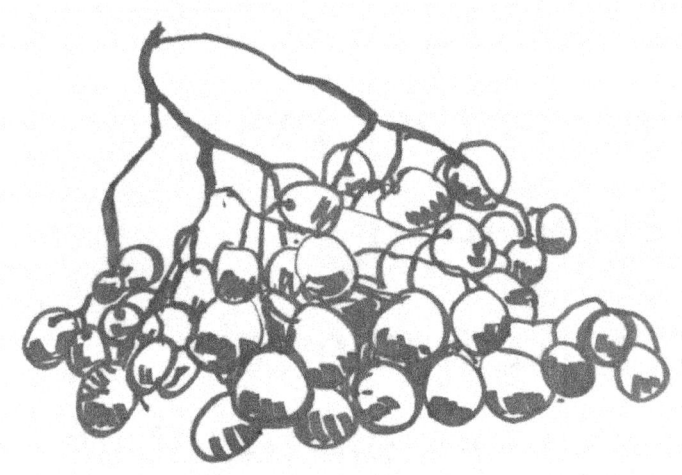

Art is too big

a gift to

undervalue.

Art is too big

a gift to

undervalue.

There are too many benefits from doing art to give up on it.

The desire to do art is already within you.

It is a gift and you are amazingly rich with gifts just by being a human being.

You just need to clean out all the negative clutter that keeps these gifts from your awareness.

Art is a friend
that will never
leave you.

It is for everyone.

And it's too much
fun not to do.

HAPPY ART-MAKING TO ALL!

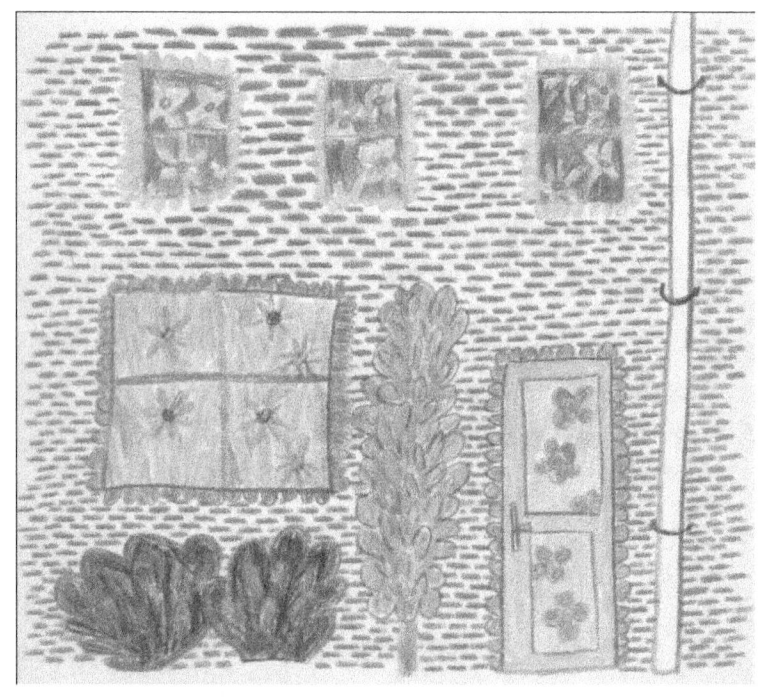

Please contact me with comments or questions through my website:

www.soliverquilling.co.uk

Recommended Books:

- *The Artist's Way* by Julia Cameron
- *Life, Paint and Passion* by Michell Cassou and Stewart Cubley

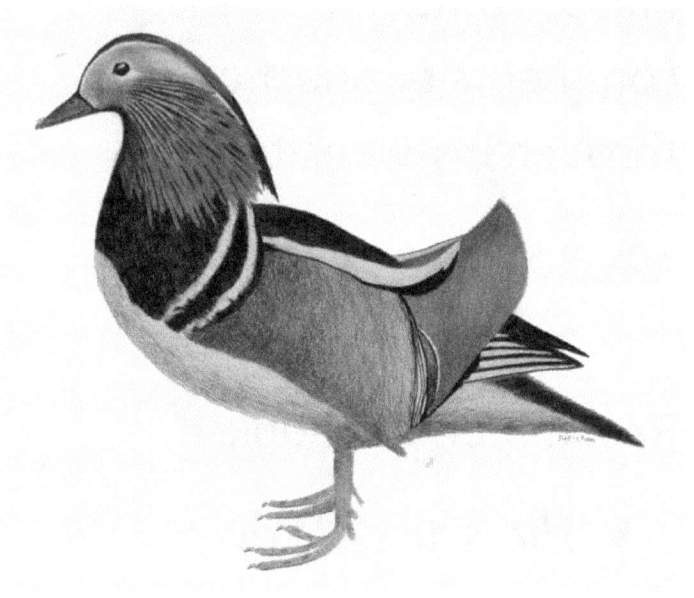

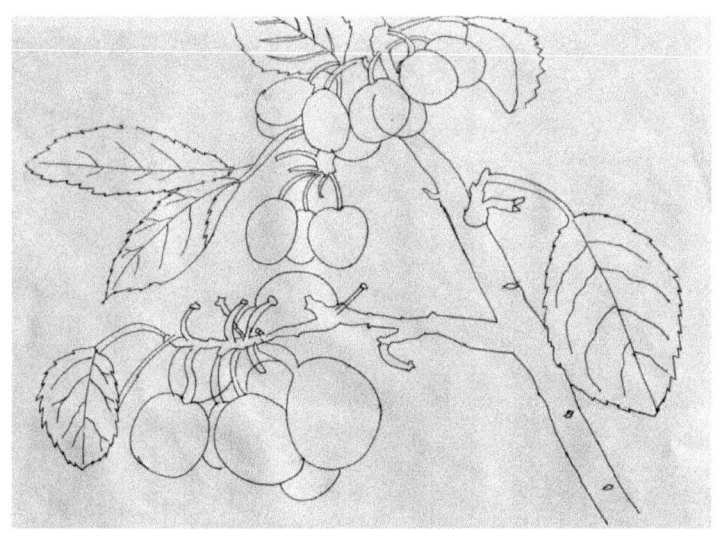

www.ingramcontent.com/pod-product-compliance
Lightning Source LLC
Chambersburg PA
CBHW071422180526
45170CB00001B/189